Dedicated to:

Mario F. Malo, my love, my life.
He shared Tudors with me and gifted Zuli to me.
Alongside of him, I have more love and joy in my life!
Thank you to my lovely Melissa, the Illustrator, who captured the
beauty and life in the story about Tudors and Zuli.
Thank you Valeria Sarmiento for bringing my dream to life.
I also want to express my gratitude to my son Matthew,
my family and close friends for their support and encouragement.

Enjoy!
Thank You!
Tudor & Zuli
Karen Herrera

No part of this publication may be reproduced
in whole or in part, or stored in a retrieval
system, electronic, mechanical, photocopying,
recording, or otherwise, without written
permission of the author.

Follow us on:

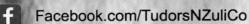

Facebook.com/TudorsNZuliCo

Instagram @tudors.n.zuli

Twitter @Tudors_N_Zuli

The Tale of Tudors and Truly Zuli

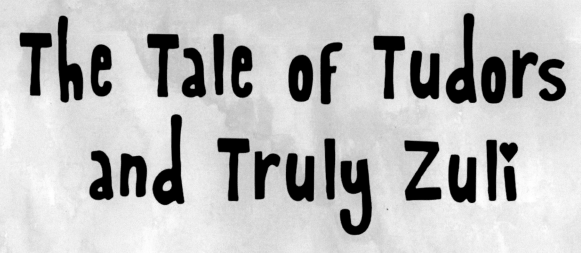

Written by
Karen Herrera

Illustrated by
La Melissa Herrera

Dog Photography by
Karen Herrera

Hello...
My name is

Tudors.

I am a four year old Maltese, and I am going to have my third and last litter of puppies!

Karen and Mario, my parents, are very excited.

There is hustle and bustle
around Karen's office today,
it is Valentine's Day.

Flowers, cards, and candy
are being given to all of Karen's
friends, but she is NOT sad.

She is sure that I am going
to have my puppies tonight...

I hope she is right.

Mario has the BEST surprise ever...
one of my adorable puppies!

Karen told her friends at work
that she is getting a precious
Maltese puppy for her Valentine's
Day gift!

I am excited to be part of her Happy Day!

It is getting dark....

Karen and Mario are home.
They give me my daily loves,
hugs, and kisses.

I fancy the attention!

Oh!

I feel movement in my tummy.

Can it be, the puppies are on their way?

Karen is thrilled!

Mario gets some blankets, puts soft music on and the puppies begin to be born...

Mario and Karen have to help me...
A baby girl puppy is born, then
a sweet little boy puppy! Oh my
goodness, we are exhausted.

Karen and Mario sit with me and
tell me that I did a GREAT job!
Both puppies are promised
to loving homes.

Karen wants to keep a female
but ... It isn't meant to be.
She is sad but smiles, gives me
pets and thanks me for being
so brave.

A while later they go off to bed.

During the night, before the clock strikes midnight, I feel a flutter inside my tummy.

What?

Another tiny baby girl puppy comes into the world.

It is a miracle!

I cuddle her up and we fall back to sleep!

Early the next morning, Karen jumps out of bed and looks inside my basket, she counts the puppies ... and to her surprise there is an EXTRA ONE!

She runs down the hallway calling to Mario, he is just as puzzled!

They both begin to laugh with delight.

Karen's puppy has been born!

They name her Zuli, the Valentine's Day puppy!

Zuli just needed a little extra time with me before entering the world.

She is the runt of the litter...

Sweet little Zuli is mine and Mario's Special Valentine gift of love to Karen.

She is "Truly Zuli" doing things her own unique way!

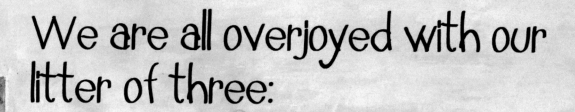

We are all overjoyed with our litter of three:

Rosie, Romie
and
Truly Zuli.

Karen says that the puppies have "Puppy Power," a joyful feeling that comes over all the people they meet.

They put a smile on every face and warmth in their hearts.

Oh my, how time flies...

The puppies not only walk and roll,
they can jump now too!

I see my little Truly Zuli playing
in the garden getting into mischief!

Oh, what garden adventures await her...

This is a VERY SPECIAL page
for you to draw a picture of your pet.
Loves, hugs and kisses from
Tudors and Truly Zuli.

cat

bageru

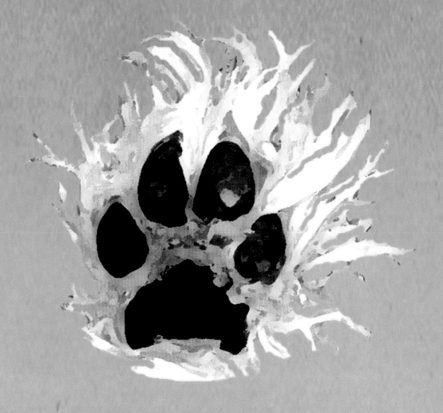

The End

Karen has many artistic talents. She has been crafty all her life and recently launched her online jewelry store - KMaloCreations.com. Over the years Tudors has brought so much light into Karen's life. Once Zuli was born, Karen felt an overwhelming sense of indescribable love. The Tale of Tudors and Truly Zuli came to her one day while she was refelcting on how the dogs fill her heart with delight. From the beginning Karen knew she wanted her daughter to illustrate the book.

Melissa, her daughter, is a passionate artist. Her favorite way to express herself is through painting. After graduating from college, she finally had the time to focus on the paitnings for the book. At last, the mother-daughter duo was able to collaborate and bring Karen's dream to life. The illustrations that make up this masterpiece are a combination of scenes from Karen's actual home and Melissa's imagination. The dogs in the paintings are real images taken by Karen.

They are both thrilled to have completed this project together and hope their creation brings happiness to all who read it.

Made in the USA
Columbia, SC
13 November 2018